MW00627386

Born on 29 July 1977, to lecturer Sam Coker and Cuisinier extraordinaire Maria Kone Coker, 'Bella Nzewi began her writing career at the age of ten. Her first book, though never published, was carefully typed by her doting and ever-encouraging mother and was titled *James and His Monkey*.

She never wrote another book from that moment until now.

To the Holy Spirit without Whom the inspiration to write will not be there; and to my best friend Meki (Jr).

'Bella Nzewi

SEASONS OF ANTIBES

AUSTIN MACAULEY PUBLISHERS™

LONDON • CAMBRIDGE • NEW YORK • SHARJAH

A CIP catalogue record for this title is available from the British Library.

ISBN 9781398447073 (Paperback)
ISBN 9781398447080 (Hardback)
ISBN 9781398447097 (ePub e-book)

www.austinmacauley.com

First Published 2023
Austin Macauley Publishers Ltd®
1 Canada Square
Canary Wharf
London
E14 5AA

All rules for study are summed up in this one:
Learn only to create.

– F.W. Joseph Schelling

Prologue

To this day I have not known why I have been called to this wonderful vocation until I made the effort to read the words of a journal written about Pliny the Elder.

Originally drawn to the script by my curiosity about the Ephraimite tribe of Israel, my vague but interesting method of research made me stumble upon his name because of his association with the court of Alexander the Great. Because he was a writer in the courts of the founder of modern-day Greece—because of his great conquests and the reported influence he had on another great leader, Julius Caesar—this led me to the genuine belief that the written word (even as the Bible attests: as in the written word) was very necessary for the capture and documentation of details that would otherwise have gone unnoticed.

I am a writer, not because I have any published work or because I am an authority on any subject, but simply because I am an observer. I think by this very nature I have likened myself to any other human being placed on the Earth by God to carefully observe my space in time and capture it for posterity, whether that be simply for my family members yet unborn to be able to enjoy through my words, which hopefully will be supported throughout this book by wonderful pictures

I have taken in this beautiful region of the world, or for you random reader, who has happened on the writings of a very interesting mind like yours. It is my avid hope that this piece of writing will allow you to glorify God in the absolute awesomeness of His creation.

Part 1

Chapter 1

"The future belongs to those who believe in the beauty of their dreams."

– Eleanor Roosevelt

No truer words but these could ever have been spoken about my time here and now. After a year of living in France, specifically in the PACA: Cote d' Azur region, I still feel as if I am in a sweet dream. I went for a meditative walk along the sandy beach last week, hoping to get an hour of exercise, but I was surprised by how the beauty of the trees – I noticed from afar – drew me continuously through windy streets, away from the edge of the coast and the noisy vacationers enjoying the last rays of sun before the autumn season, into the heart of Antibes, through neighbourhoods I had no idea existed, and schools I had only seen as I passed by in buses. Being careful not to stop at Place de Gaulle, I followed the distant mountain view trying to get my mind ever closer to God as I listened to the Abide App I had just downloaded. The beautiful garden chime helped to draw my attention to the smell of the morning and makes me notice for the first time how crisp the air really gets as you climb higher.

Suddenly my legs feel tired and for the first time in a while I feel the urge to sit and relax for a moment. I look around and notice I am in a strange neighbourhood, that I had not travelled all my bus routes through, and trust me, dear reader, I have gone on many bus rides in my one year here.

So, I take some pictures and in the distance, I see the Cap d'Antibes. I hadn't realised that I had circumvented the other part of Juan Les Pins from along the beach, through the beginning of Boulevard Wilson and veering off into Antibes. It had taken the better part of non-stop walking (save to pray, meditate by recording the waves for five minutes, and stretch intermittently) for about 144 minutes.

The houses I see remind me of the times I was a little girl and took a bicycle ride within the Shell Estate in Warri, the city of my birth. That night I had got home where my brother, sister and I were staying with an aunt and I dreamt of having the lives of the predominantly Dutch staff who had come to live and work at the 'Ogunu' camp as it was popularly called in those days. My memory isn't great, but knowing myself, I must have thought that one day I, too, would be in a place like this, just sitting there looking around. I noticed that most homes were probably furnished in the same way I had seen those Dutch homes furnished so many years ago when that image was imprinted inside my head. The mind is a wonderful place! For me it is like nature in that it is bare vegetative soil and can be prepared to sprout whatever seeds you place in it. Carefully nurtured, they bring forth fruits and plants and flowers to create a very beautiful garden of thoughts, those thoughts are lived out in experiences that materialise and push us to our reality, and if we are one of the lucky ones who notice or take the time to ponder like you are doing by reading this book, you too will understand that you at this moment are living the dream you dreamt perhaps last night, two weeks ago or even 30 years ago.

Chapter 2

"But now they desire a better country, that is, a heavenly:
wherefore God is not ashamed to be called their God: for He
had prepared for them a city."

– Hebrews 11:16

It rained heavily last night, and looking out at the sky this morning, I can clearly see the stars. I feel that they are all aligning in the right moment of my life. The early morning sky is so dark and since the clouds drained themselves out, the stars are shining so brightly that I can see them.

Your hand is in this, I say to God; For the past 12 months, I've been more aware of a friend I didn't realise I had—the Holy Spirit—some may call it a ghost. He paves the way for every step I make and to Him first I must give ALL credit as my true inspiration.

The day is dark, and the early morning breeze is cold and chilly, biting into my knees, but I am determined to hear the first train pass, so I sit out here with my mug of freshly brewed coffee and my jotter and pen (for my laptop is charging because I awoke at about 2 am in a state of total paralysis, not knowing where to begin the novel). However, starting anywhere as Bruce Mau advised got me to one thousand and six words typed and a completely drained writing processor. So, I focus my mind on the chirping of the birds all around this domain of flowers, this secret garden where my apartment in Juan Les Pins is tucked to the right, looking into the hills of Cannes at a distance and to the left the Cap d'Antibes. From my balcony, I can see the outline of the pool, and in the far distance imagine hearing the roaring of the waves as they gently hit the shoreline of the beach. Once again, I am so grateful to my friend who led my footsteps to this place, and in this moment I'm reminded of a verse which speaks of another country, of a sect of people who imagined a place so long ago before it had ever been spoken about, and to them it was apportioned as faith. What a word: faith. It's very hard to have faith when one cannot see, so I like to stick with the angel that says show me your faith and I will show you my works. It was F. W. Schelling that said, "Nature is visible spirit; spirit is invisible nature..." How may I imagine something or somewhere I have never seen? However, out here in Antibes Les Pins, my imagination is suddenly awakened, I can see what those fathers of our faith imagined as they walked the beautiful Earth and deserts and sometimes got stranded in seas. For all of nature, indeed, is awesome and everything around us, if ONLY we are careful to notice speaks of and points to this country. One of the key founding principles of our study in geology states that: "The present is the key to the past." So looking around the mountains that surround me in Les Templiers, where I often sit to write, meditate and jot down my little gratitude prayers, I imagine this country, taking a closer look of this beautiful gift presented to me, which I shall try to expose as we journey through the city of Antibes allows me to imagine the beauty spoken of in Revelation, one of the most compelling literary works of ancient times. Sometimes understanding and looking at the past helps us unlock the future. In the future, there will be a city that will not need the sun (the actual centre of our solar system) and the moon (which for centuries had been the constant debate for astronomers) because the glory of God will be the light, and the lamb (Jesus Christ) will be light we need. I can imagine that easily, because now as the morning light penetrates the dark sky I see only the blue hue on the sky, and so this makes me understand that what we see is only a perception of our minds and the reflection of light. In less than an hour of staying here, I can see that so clearly. The skies were never dark at all to begin with, the stars never leave the sky, but rather what happens between day and night is that the mind is played on by the reflection of the light that we see. The sun covers the darkness and the moon enlightens it. Everything is a reflection of what is between the heavens, and we can only see what God wants us to see. He will not be ashamed to sit on the throne of the new city, but that does not mean He is not sitting on the throne right now. As a matter of fact, He actually sits on the throne of every heart that has allowed Christ to be in him/her.

When I think of preparation, I sometimes consider the way we prepare ourselves as a parent for our new-born. We go all out to prepare the baby's room, and depending on the sex of that baby, we paint the room to reflect the gender. Some go all blue or red for boys and pink to purple for girls depending on the preference of the parent. God says I go to prepare a city for you. Jesus says if it were not so I would not tell you, and if I go then I will come back to gather you to Myself.

By the time the baby comes into this beautiful room, he/she is actually colourblind and knows not what you have taken extreme pain to prepare. Sometimes this is the way of the new Christian, absolutely clueless to the extent the Father has gone to prepare the city for him/her to ensure that we all can enter. I consider my time in Antibes with much gratitude, simply because I recall one morning as I sat by the beach near the apartment, I noticed a big truck coming towards me, and I hadn't realised until I noticed its purpose was to clean the beach area, and that beaches needed to be cleaned too; to this day I am amazed when all over the city very early in the morning you hear the workers in their trucks cleaning the roads, the beaches and all the surroundings so that everywhere looks clean and smells nice. This is totally not what I am accustomed to in my country, though I remember going once for a tournament in Lomé, Togo and early in the morning I would always awaken to the noise of government workers sweeping and cleaning the roads in the morning; they did it once it was 5 pm in the evening too.

Definitely this must be something in the French culture: beauty and the appreciation of order and cleanliness, for indeed the Juan Les Pins beaches are one of the cleanest I have ever seen in my life. Cleanliness, a form of godliness indeed, for the good book says, "and beside this, giving all diligence, add to your faith virtue; and to virtue knowledge; and to knowledge temperance; and to temperance patience; and to patience godliness; and to godliness brotherly kindness; and to brotherly kindness LOVE."

These are the steps to the kingdom in a nutshell hidden in the Gospel but thoroughly spelled out by the Apostle Peter in his first letter. Peter was a faithful brother, and my prayer is that, just as he took Jesus' instruction as He was leaving to feed His flock, I, and each and every one of us, will take seriously the injunction given to us as believers to encourage one another. In France and in the cleanliness of my surroundings, I have slowly but surely come to understand the meaning of these few lines of Peter in a way that no other could have been able to explain to me. By calling me out here, the Holy Spirit has made me, to literally lie in green pastures, literally restored my soul and allowed me to know and see Him, just for His name's sake and no other reason, that I may raise a hallelujah like so many who have walked on these sand beaches have done before me.

It is only when we fully know Jesus and see Him as He truly is that we can fully know and be seen as we truly are. In their 1999 comedy-drama, Bruce Willis and Michelle Pfeiffer portrayed the need in each of us to be seen, and one of the best lines in that movie for me was when Kate said, "There is a history here…" What she was actually saying to Ben was, "I see you!" We see God when we see all the others around us. We see God when we thank Him for all the beauty that we see around us.

If you have ever loved anyone at all – a parent, a child, a boyfriend, or girlfriend or spouse – then you surely have seen God! It is a fully compassing feeling, not only on the outside that makes your pants wet (guys, you know what I mean) or that make your hearts flutter ladies, as if you would have a heart attack or go out of breath or remain speechless when the object of your affection walks into a room; or the silent content feeling you get when a child says thank you for a day well spent with them or for a meal thoughtfully prepared, or when a friend says, "Thank you for thinking of me," you hit the spot! All these are expressions and feelings of agape love and eros love: but for me the one that stands out the most is the meeting of hearts and mind, when in silence just watching a movie, attending a concert, sharing the same space in a room together reading without speaking or sitting on a dining table on a warm afternoon with the sun on your face, enjoying a meal and you can connect in conversation. These are the moments when you know God. For He can be found in the eyes of the one sitting across from you; the one who pauses to see you and frees you to be yourself. In those eyes, you have met with God. You have spoken to Him, you have touched His hands and seen the twinkle of a smile so beautiful it warms the insides of your heart and calms you like the oceans water. Like the calming waves when they hit the beach line as you walk along the beach.

God places an idea in our minds and causes us to work on it with Him if we allow. It is as if He is saying to us: I am with you my dear one and I want you to know it! In sharing our ideas with Him, we are one with God, and He allows us to follow Him in a way we can connect. It is powerful because it is a choice we make and we give power to when we share

23

these thoughts and ideas with others like us around the world and hence know for sure that good is at work to overcome evil on a much larger scale around the world. For light cannot be hidden under a table; it must shine and the world must know it, for His word says: "...I shall be exalted in the nations. I shall be glorified on the Earth." Doing the will of God doesn't mean we need to be perfect, rather it implies that we need to lean on the comforter and helper which is the Holy Spirit to guide us into the good that we must do, like Christ, we find ourselves irreproachable – blameless – like God made us in Christ when He took the sin of the world on His shoulders and nailed it to the cross. We must choose not to listen to the devil but understand that we can be weak and yet be very strong, for as Moses realised many times in his exodus journey that it was always at the moments he felt the weakest, that God showed His strength which is not yet anywhere near His strongest.

Dear reader, even though Christ testified that He was greater than John the Baptist, I believe the best is yet to come for those of us who are now Christians. We are strong when we recognise that He dwells within us and that the great ideas we have, when acted upon to do our brother good and to take care of ourselves—that is, to guard our hearts and minds—to the point where we are not side-tracked by every gossip about the other to bring about strife that saps our energy, then collectively we are able to truly love one another and are closer to bringing about the greatness we seek.

Ideas come always in Coffee Shops

Chapter 3

"And the nations of them which are saved shall walk in the light of it: and the kings of the earth do bring their glory and honour into it."

– Revelations 21;24

Now that I am no longer green in this place, I know that today, Friday, November 1st, is a public holiday. Last year at this time my daughter and I had ventured out on a rainy day to visit Place de Gaulle and at least do some shopping while spending a beautiful daughter/mother time bonding in our new environment. I was eager to show off Juan Les Pins and my beautiful Place de Gaulle. I showed her the poem I had written about this lovely place the first month after I had gotten there and also wanted to show off the Picasso Museum next to the Cathedral. Plus, I wanted her to sit with me and read in the little English bookstore that I had discovered. Literature is something she and I share, so imagine my disappointment when we got there and all the shops were closed. And it was so cold and rainy that having the only shop open be the English bookstore should have been a sign to me that I should have actually been spending more time there than I have in this past year.

Writing this book gives me the excuse I need to sit still and just read and research, which is what I have been doing all day this day too. I went back or should I say rather that I was led to the place in Nice where it all began about five years ago heading for a work seminar in Norway after attending the November parents-teachers' meeting at the tennis academy where my first daughter attended. Then, I had decided to stop in the Malongo Coffee Shop along Jean Medecin, one of the famous streets in Nice to have a last cup of coffee before catching the train to the airport—and dream.

Looking down from the Columbus Café on the 3rd floor today, I notice right in front of me the Notre Dame Cathedral and it seemed that it was yesterday I had been inside praying for an opportunity to live in the south of France. Having that cup of coffee so many years ago, thinking of streets filled with people browsing the shops seemed like something that I could, for the moment, dream of and now in my reality I see myself doing just that almost every other day. I watch the people and often wonder how their lives are? A game I like to play often as I wait for the bus or sip a cup of coffee is the 'guess what they are saying game'. In this place of creativity, the thoughts are mine and I fill them based on whatever gestures I observe on the faces of two people walking along the street. More often than not I always notice the lonely ones and I ask myself: "Are they so lonely because they have no one in their lives to be with or is it that they have driven those that love them away by their own attitudes?"

Leading to the Cap d'Antibes

Whatever the case may be, the reality is that there are quite a lot of lonely souls walking the streets today. People are desperate for connections and sometimes looking for them in the wrong places like Facebook and/or Instagram. I definitely am not averse to any of these phantoms of technology but at least I know the purpose they serve and hence use them as such and not as a substitute for meaningful relationships. Why, I ask myself, are likes more important to a person's evaluation or expectations of themselves? Why do some offer explanations to complete strangers and are ready to divulge deep secrets to the world that they are not willing to share to their immediate loved ones? As if when these things come out in the open it will not be read by the very ones who should have known it in the first place. Daunting as this may be I decided a long time ago that if I were in a room full of people who just decide to be on their phones the whole time, then the next time they ask me out I will politely decline, so they know that if I do spend time with you, I expect at least the courtesy of your quality time with me discussing those little bits of nothing that make life really interesting (smile). Now back to the beauty of Antibes, I think that was enough digression on the ills of our present media crazy new age.

Place de Gaulle: A square in the heart of the centre of Antibes, a place that captivated me so much in the first year that I was inspired to write a few lines of how I felt and it goes thus – has anywhere so captured your imagination it seems almost unreal and electrifying at the same time? Unreal because you don't believe that a singular place can evoke such emotions within you, and electrifying because of the feeling of being so alive that it keeps drawing you to its fountain of life each time.

Fountain of life: this is what Jesus describes Himself to the lady he meets at the well, and has a very interesting conversation with. In an instant, he summarises her life for her and she is truly amazed; rather than making her feel ashamed, his words exposes her in depths that caress and make her love Him so much so, and she wants others to love Him as she does. Immediately she runs back home and brings her friends with her to meet this stranger – friend who is definitely like no other. There is a definite glow and attraction about Him that she finds too hard to explain, but at the same time she cannot contain, and it must be shared. Now this is exactly how I feel about Antibes Les Pins and especially about Place de Gaulle. It can look like a different place each season of the year and wears its leaves in all the amazing colours of each season. For now, as we enter into the season of fall/autumn depending on which part of the world you are reading this, the leaves of the trees which just a couple of months ago were fresh green and overgrowing, are beginning just now to turn brownish yellow and with every slight breeze that blows through falls to the ground. Soon I know as we head into winter and with the first sights of the snow on the peak of the Alps, you will begin to notice that these same trees will have leaves that are as white as the snow that you see cover the mountains in the far distance.

This past May I had a friend visiting and I convinced her to come with me to this magical place with the fountains that spring forth water from the pavements that are swept every morning. Between the Paul and Sarah Baker shops where customers line up for coffee, baguettes and freshly baked brioche, there is never a stop to the buzz of the place. Electrifying I say, simply magnifique! I want to share this place with all my friends, I want them to feel as I feel in this place and I feel much obliged to do so with you, my reader.

Allow yourself to sit in a coffee shop every day for a week or two if you have the luxury of time, and experiment with that one idea that has been simmering in the back of your mind for ages. You have tried desperately to let it go, but still it holds you. It shows up in your dreams when you go to sleep and wakes you up sometimes when you least expect it. Moreover, you find that the universe, in some odd way, keeps bringing it back in the words of strangers like me. Yes, that is the thought I'd like you to take with you to the coffee shop or if tea is your preference, sit out there and let it brew.

There is always time for Coffee

Part 2:
Bury the Demons?

Psalm 139

Chapter 4

"So, my friends, I choose to be an eagle and fly so far away that when I come back I may see what the Holy Spirit has done in my stead."

— Excerpts from a letter to my 42-year-old self.

It's raining again here this morning and I guess these months from October to November are the only times in 12 months that this area gets its heaviest rainfall. I love to sit on my sofa and stare out the glass-door looking past the immediate balcony to the hills of Golfe Juan, the village next door; it makes me imagine Cannes, which is only a 15-minute drive from Juan Les Pins. I don't know why but since I moved here I have been so captivated by the city of Cannes, so much so that I always make sure to go there at least twice every month just to look around.

We've been promised about five inches of precipitation today in Antibes/Biot, so definitely yes! As I can see from my comfy spot, the pounding rain and thunderstorms, this is indeed the rainy season of Antibes Les Pins!

With coffee in hand this Sunday morning, I reflect on the letter I have written to my 42-year-old self, thinking that if the creator and Jehovah Rophe keeps me healthy I shall read it on my 85th birthday and ponder on what I was thinking at this moment:

Dear Self,

I'm learning a language. I'm learning a culture – a new way of doing things. I'm battling injury and a new life style. I'm trying to be the best mother and mental coach to my 12-year-old son, and maintaining a long-distance relationship with my husband of 21 years, at the same time trying to let go of my children (21 and 19) so as to develop a new relationship with them as daughters; as they walk this lovely but yet sometimes turbulent times of becoming their own WOMEN. I dare not think of myself even now, for to pause and contemplate that may throw me into such a frenzy that I am afraid I may not recover from. So, my friends, I choose to be an EAGLE and fly so far away that when I come back I may see what the Holy Spirit has done in my stead. He promises that I will run and not go weary, I will walk and shall not faint, to this promise I hold on for God truly is not man that He should lie! He has sworn by two things which must happen first before His word will be something to doubt, one by the day and night, and the other by the ordinances of Heaven and Earth.

And so, I hope as I continue to hold onto His promises that are yeah and amen, every morning I shall contemplate and praise Him for His blessings that are new every day. Yesterday is surely gone and be it the best or worst day of your life, believe it or not it won't matter come the morning because with the passing of one night comes the dawn of another day better and brighter than the last; if only you and I would pause to see the maker's hands as He carefully sculpts the tapestry of our lives woven into the canvass of His divine, unique and well-constructed universe. Our lives all intertwined unbeknownst to us, but living daily as pilgrims we who walk as Abraham did, a sojourner in the land, as Isaac did, a peace loving man who would rather walk away from the sweat of his hands than lay a hand on the ones who kept his father for so long, as Jacob who fought God, even when he knew he didn't deserve to have a blessing, for a blessing he sought; not allowing the lie of the devil to murky his eyes or cloud his judgements but laying claim to the promise of his Grandfather Abraham he went as far as Egypt so his sons would be preserved until it was time to inherit the land that had been promised so long ago. If we all could pause for a moment and learn from the seasons of our lives and those of the witnesses that surround us, we would but see the part of the universe that we are meant to witness; and if for a moment we pause long enough, the Holy Spirit in His kindness may lead us indeed to see that for which our generation was meant to learn from us and then we could truly say that our lives are fit for purpose. For me at this time and season I find myself in a beautiful land, amidst people of faith and hope. They may not know God as I do, but still He teaches them for that is His work and the work of the Holy Spirit remaining and tarrying until the time for judgement. I see in those around me the hope of a generation. Mothers believing and sacrificing because of their kids and the talent in them. Fathers with hard sweat giving the fruit of their labour to provide an education and a vocation so that their children may reap where they have sown. With blood, sweat and tears frontiers are being pushed and barriers broken so that those who are unseen may truly become seen. For only when they see us, can the hidden works of our hands be established as His words have promised. So, in those words I stand now in this season of hibernation. In winter when the world sleeps around me and the animals conserve heat and energy and the trees turn brown and lose their leaves I know indeed it is a time to sow and be still, and know that He is God!

If the stars and seasons still obey Him, then so will I. If the heavens and all that is in them follow a definite timetable it means that my life too is on His radar and my time like all of us who truly believe in Him will have our times of refreshing. So as the rains fall, let it! As the clouds darken and the storm rages on let it! For as sure as the night comes and then the morning so also will the sun come out again!!!

Hope you have a good life my dear; for now, I must go to living until we see in due time.

It is I.

Much love,

Self.

Recently I went to the theatre in Antibes to watch the play *Hamlet* by Shakespeare and was reminded by one of the characters, Polonius, of this statement: "This above all: to thine own self be true. And it must follow, as the night the day, thou canst not then be false to any man." Well, we all know what befell that family; but now starkly contrast that with the teaching of Jesus in Mark saying to his disciples: "If anyone would come after me, he must deny himself and take up his cross and follow me." Today we talk about what is referred as a paradigm shift, like as though it were a new concept, when in actual fact Jesus came in order that we should have a paradigm shift in our lives. The change from the OLD self to the NEW-BORN AGAIN is the biggest paradigm shift that we can ever imagine or explain.

The Holy Spirit is the ONLY person that can facilitate that to happen in the life of the believer. However, for this to take effect, there must be a willingness to repent and acknowledge that we all have demons that must be expunged from our deepest beings. Now some of this process is what gentlemen like Bob Proctor and Napoleon Hill have spent their life work to expound.

Burying the demons is what a lot of us have done, when what we should actually focus our attention on teaching others is the expunging of the demon and replacing it with transforming our minds by the word of God. We must have the courage to add VIRTUE to our faith when we become born-again Christians: what do I mean? We should be courageous enough to have a true conversation with ourselves and the Holy Spirit (*because there are some deeply buried demons that we don't know exist until He shows it up for us*) and allow the cleansing power and blood of Jesus to wash it off and make it clean as snow, then once that is done we must not allow idleness or emptiness to take control because that allows the demon to come back with friends and even take a stronger hold, rather we should hold unto the one idea from the last chapter and work on it with ALL excellence. Throwing into this the same effort we did with the former. I am optimistic this is possible that we have the power to do this because of the Holy Spirit in us. This is what I have come to see more clearly in this time in Antibes. He is in me and I am in Him. The expression of which F. W. Schelling said for nature is invisible spirit!

So, in some ways, I must be true to myself, but to which self? The old? Certainly not for that old self, which has low self-esteem and has not been linked with the highest possible power available on this Earth since creation for us men to walk in. We are meant to be the dominant ones in the equation and our dominance should be seen in the way we manage the elements around us. Man tries to go about it the wrong way most of the time, and this is the reason why it has been murky and blurry for mankind for so long that we don't even see the hand writing on the wall. It started of course since before ancient of days and for as long as we have been programmed we forgot the way the equation was for humans; however, in reminding ourselves to be correct from within, when we but rest and take time to observe the animals and nature all around us, we can then come back to the way it should be, which is that we dominate in a respectful controlling way, like you would a garden or an animal farm, and love those who are around us. We are in no way asked to manage people, we are not asked to control and manipulate others so that our self is satisfied, rather the creator asks only one thing from us that we respect and control the Earth He has so wonderfully made for us and love and encourage each other. We are to treat one another even as we would love to be treated and finally we are to look out for those who are less privileged than we are, not as a means to subjugate or boast, but as the ultimate passage for us to become more like Him who created us, so that as we can be more of our spiritual selves and groan for the body that He will present us with, which will allow man to live in the place Christ promised to prepare for us.

You see I truly believe in the proclamation statement Bob Proctor repeats in so many of his seminars: "...I am God's highest form of creation..." sometimes listening to this over and over again in my own voice allows me to believe deep down within myself in meditation. Most times the battle is half-won when we can take care of the person on the inside. Recently, while on vacation an incidence that happened in a room close to mine sprung up a demon deep inside that I had no idea was still lodged in. The experience led me to face it and give a name to the emotion that it evoked and in doing that I was able to face the feelings raised – mostly negative – but more than that it brought me face to face to my one idea once more, and allowed me to make a bold statement on how I was going to utilise that passion to help others. If I had not been aware of the Holy Spirit in my life and listening to the guidance that He freely offers to those who listen, then I probably would not have had the epiphany brought about by the expunging of that false belief of myself. I let go of something that I knew I should have let go a long time ago and opened a very healthy and revealing conversation with those who were connected to me at the time I was born; however, what I really needed to understand from the vacation experience was that at the time of my rebirth, I had been separated from my mother's womb and transported into the kingdom of light. Being AWARE of this can come only from my declaration of it; first to myself and then to others. Nicodemus, who sought Jesus at night, could not understand this, but Paul who became an Apostle by the Spirit of God acknowledges and proclaims this in his letter to the Galatians by saying: "But when it pleased God, who separated me from my mother's womb, and called me by His grace…" Notice here that the separation and the calling are two different things: In acts 22:21 he re-confirms that calling but also was confirmed when the Lord stood by Him and said in Acts 23:11 – "Be of good cheer, Paul: for as thou has testified of me in Jerusalem, so must thou bear witness also at Rome."

What an assurance!

As my eyes become more open to the Holy Spirit's work in me, I realise that with each passing day, I am becoming a different person, first and foremost broken and humbled, and knowing that I cannot help myself, I cling to the Holy Spirit, my comforter and helper, thereby tapping into the great energy. I can do everything through His strength alone. Following this, I abandon my old self and cast away the things that hold me back. How do I do this? Indeed, by a mental transformation and renewal.

Who has seen the mind?

Transforming from the inside out...

The time at the Beachcomber watching the Nadal Match

Chapter 5

*"O praise the Lord all ye nations: praise Him all ye people.
For His merciful kindness is great towards us: and the truth
of the Lord endureth forever. Praise ye the Lord!"*

– Psalm 117

What is truth? I hear this phrase 'truth be told...' said a
lot. And more often than not, what is said next is the person's
perception of a matter or his or her point of view on
something. But my dear inquisitive reader, congratulations for
staying with this book this far. I truly am grateful and
honoured that you would read even past the most difficult
subjects to some, and for that I feel compelled to tell you what
truth is – it is whatever the Lord says it is – and I am in awe
because as I sit here in France when I look all around me what
I see is the majesty of creation. Within six days, God created
the world, and afterwards He rested and said looking at His
works that it was perfect. Sitting here in Biot, which is just
some fifteen minutes distance by car to Antibes Les Pins
where I reside, and on the drive from there to here I have to
come through a roundabout facing one of the most

magnificent mountains that I have ever seen: I reflect on the drive towards this mountain today and remember how awestruck I was, thinking to myself, this same time last year these mountains had already begun to spot some snow on their peaks. So, the question that arose in my mind was: What has happened in the past one year that has caused a change? Why now 4/11/2019 is it impossible to see the snow-capped mountain, a signal that one season is ending and another just about to creep in? If I said truth be told there is climate change, that is something that will take perhaps decades for some to accept, and then again it may cause a whole lot of debates; also, if I were to say that mothers love their kids and if someone were to try to kill any one of our kids or a wild animal were to come to the park where we were taking a walk we would do anything in our power to save that kid and not allow harm come to the child, yes? However, though that be the truth, it is also unfortunately quite debatable because we know that in this sick world there are even some who would sell their kids to slavery, sex and drugs or sacrifice them on the altar or to a black magician (babalawo) just to improve their livelihoods. So, truth be told… In some real-life situations could be relatively arguable.

For me the one truth that is absolutely unarguable is the one I find in John 10:28 – 29. For the first time, I know for a certainty that even if it is arguable by some certain 'intelligent' people you will NEVER find it not being true. The verses reads: "…and I give unto them eternal life; and they shall never perish, neither shall any man pluck them out of my hand. My Father which gave them me, is greater than all, and no man is able to pluck them out of my Father's hand."

Jesus loves us too MUCH! Now that's a truth be told.

In this beautiful place, I can see you face to face. When I look to the east, I see the trees and the wind blows them so that I praise Your holy name with a melody in my heart and sway in my feet; and to the west is the beach the wonderful blue waters of Juan Les Pins, and looking further down are the Islands of St Tropez, I think. Walking within the domain where I live is one of the best kept flower gardens one could ever imagine, sometimes I wonder if this was just specifically made for me, because I honestly believe that even the famous Eleanor Roosevelt gardens will have a real competition on their hands if they were compared on one of those TV garden shows. Anyway, considering that I try to take late evening walks just listening to and observing the garden vibes, makes me come face to face with you. Jesus I love, I say sometimes out loud. I sit on the small fence and ponder on some of the Psalms, reciting a particular verse over and over with great gratitude in my heart, I say, "What is there not to be thankful for!"

It is this grateful attitude, I must admit, that keeps me sane in the face of the life trials I have faced in the last 12 months. Not trying to play the victim card but seeing beauty in everything around me and asking God for the privilege of another day to sip a cup of coffee in the morning makes me so joyful! Coffee drinking, as you know, is part of French culture, and no other place I know does it better than Malongo Coffee Shop. If you don't believe me then why do you think in this extremely busy world where people are always in a rush, every day thousands of people wait in queue to have their cups of coffee made by a real barista who takes his time.

The beautiful blue waters of the surrounding Isles.

The freshly baked to perfection Madeleines cannot be replicated by any other shop. The ambience of the shop right next to the Notre Dame never falls short for me each time I'm there. In fact, I would definitely like to test out this theory on a wet and rainy afternoon, reading a novel and enjoying an 8€ large cup of 'Le Blue Mountain de la Jamaïque'. On the counters are lines of water cups (glass) for customers to have their customary water before and after their coffee, ensuring the acidity level of the body does not become too high as they consume their coffees. Drinking coffee has never felt as good to me as it has been in the past one year. Listening to the chatter of customers is like being in a Picasso museum and seeing all the abstract paintings coming together as one complete canvas of creativity and in me it is the perfect place to bring out my own symphonies. I'm creating words being lost in the humdrum. Like magic, my hands type out my thoughts without pausing to think: it's like I'm in a wave and being pushed and pulled deeper and deeper not particularly caring if what I'm typing is making sense or not. I'm like a child given a new toy or a drum for Christmas and all I want to do is bang and bang and bang for hours in the end knowing that or at least praying that one day I too will have a famous band and play tracks like 'Imagine Dragons' and I will tell all those neighbours who endured the noise silently for years that the torture that they had to go through was not for nothing. Such is the beauty of a place like this. But one of the actual things that amaze me is the way the coffee is served and as I wait for my second cup of the morning, listening to the chiming of the bells of the Church reminding us that another hour has passed. I imagine the words of Jesus saying to us, "Not one hair of your head drops to the ground without me knowing." If I say to myself a company on Earth can train its staff to be so meticulous over a simple cup of coffee and this allows them to make and declare profits every year, then how much more are the rewards of a God who says to me that I am more precious to Him than the birds of the air. How happy and joyful should the revelation of this word make me feel, when I hear the words that I am His workmanship created in Christ Jesus unto good works! How jubilant am I that concerning me through Paul who penned them down and the Holy Spirit that has quickened it to my understanding that it was actually in the plans of God before time that we should walk in them. Just like the leaders of the Starbucks, McDonalds and indeed Malongo have followed their leadership style and put staff through various training courses from the moment they are hired so that they work in a certain way; so also, we, who are called by Him in Christ Jesus, are made to walk in a certain way. We cannot hide it, we cannot force it, only others will see it in us and wonder what manner of people we are. It is in the wonder of this that we explain that it is not us, but we point upwards and say it is all Him. I was talking to a friend yesterday in reply to a question of – Ca Va? I reply by my gesture (since I am still learning the language) of a tennis serve position and say, "So great!" When I take up a racket and I look up into the heavens at that instant all I feel is gratitude to the creator who allows me to see the beauty both God made and man-made all around me and I shout a big hallelujah so much so that by the action goosebumps take over my body. Jesus, you love me too much!

The time at the Laser tag waiting for our Bowling Game

The Boulangerie - A Way of Life...

Chapter 6

"En ce jour-la, vous connaitrez que Je suis en Mon Pere, que vous êtes en moi, et que Je suis en vous."

– Jean 14:20

Having an experience that one cannot simply explain is a miracle in my book. It was so extraordinary that it took my breath away. Dear reader, good thing it happened today when I am stuck on day five. What exactly do you want me to call getting a free Uber ride that was extremely wonderful and had a Godly experience that I have never felt before? Before I indulge into this experience, I have to mention that actually I was going to write about the short visit I had into Nice in the morning, it was going to be one thousand words of my allotted portion for today, because I deliberately took the train into Nice to see the Pole d'Echange, Antibes. It's one of the most picturesque places to behold and one that, I have noticed, gives the first of snow, signalling the approaching winter.

From the bridge overlooking the train station, one can gaze into the distance for minutes on end—something I found myself doing a lot early this year—and not only admire the beautiful boats adorning Port Vauban, but also see the Alps in the distance! And as sure as night turns into day, and the stars still brighten up the skies at night, today I saw the snow-capped mountains that were not there just a week ago. For me, it was a sure sign that God is in His heavens holding all things in place. I reckon the rains of the past weekend must have deposited some of the snow in its wake as it brought with it some cold winds.

So back to the Uber experience, like I was saying I had gone into Mougin today—another of those beautiful mountainous cities surrounding Antibes—to have a procedure done at the Tzanck Hospital. On getting there, I decided that I would have an Uber take me back to my apartment rather than go back to my son's school, since I was sure by now that he would not be playing any tournament games that day. When I pressed the search button, I chose for the first time an Uber Comfort since I needed to stretch my legs on the journey home. It was going to be a fourteen-minute wait: since it was a lovely afternoon in Mougin I decided to wait outside rather than sit at the reception, plus I didn't want to have him drive into the hospital and have to get a ticket, so I waited outside while appreciating the beauty of the place around me, though somewhat distracted by the heaviness, I was already beginning to feel in my leg. So, I texted the driver when I noticed that he had completed his last ride and immediately he called me to ask if I was in Mougin to which I answered, "Of course." He told me in faulty English that he was on his way. Happy that at least he could communicate in English at all I was feeling a bit confident that if I had to help him find his way to the pick-up point I had chosen then it would be no problem, or at least so I thought. Trust me I have had at least one or two bad communication problems here in France that has cost me money and wasted time just waiting for a ride. But today this was not the case. Though it took us five minutes trying to figure out where he was and where I was – it was as if the man was cut out of the 'patient' tree itself (smile), while I was seething in some pain and praying desperately under my breath that he wouldn't just end the ride and drive off, I had the presence of mind to ask him if he saw a white truck (which apparently was the obstruction in his sight path and vice-versa), so once I mentioned that I was on the other side of the Rondpoint at least I was hoping that my French pronunciations were audible to him, he immediately made the turn and saw me – he was all smiles, which to me was a relief – and then I entered the car quickly and sunk into the very comfy Mercedes V-class. Now you see why I said to have that free in the first place just without the Godly experience was a bonus, right?! So, then we are on our way and he starts off by asking if I was okay and if the visit to the hospital was okay for me, to which I answered in the affirmative on both counts. Smiling I sat back and felt a bit more relaxed so much so that I asked if I could play my own music, for I just wanted to do a quiet worship session as we drove back. At this moment, he offered to ask me if I wanted to play it through the car's Bluetooth and I said why not. Considering it was religious music and not wanting to offend, for I had not noticed yet the rosary hanging on his sun-block, I asked if it was okay that my playlist was a Christian one. He said he actually loved that kind of music which made me relax an additional notch. Just what the doctor had ordered… Trying to get my phone on his car Bluetooth was beginning to be a pain, but believe me when I said that he was the epitome of patience. He kept at it and when it was apparent it wasn't going to connect on mine, he surprised me by offering to play the music through his own phone. I gave him her name and immediately at the slow down he was quickly and safely able to do a search and choose the song I wanted to hear, after a few tries (like the devil was trying hard to stop the music from playing in the car) the Bluetooth co-operated and we had the song going on in the car finally. Boy! Immediately the voice came up through the car speakers, the atmosphere exploded in some electrifying way. The sound quality was so clear it was as if the Spirit of God was using the music to speak directly to him and from nowhere – something I have never actually done in my entire life, and I must emphasise I haven't done this in my entire life – I raised my hands right there in the car and spoke directly out loud, "Father I give you all the glory, I don't know what is going on this car but whatever it is I ask that you come take full control and let your will be done…" Immediately, he said I feel like I have goosebumps in me. I knew within me that the Holy Spirit had wanted him to be the one to pick me. I knew also that no other Uber driver was meant to pick me but him and that all my prayer up until that moment was for this. All morning even when I went to the Notre Dame to pray for about 30 minutes I was conscious of the Holy Spirit's guidance, and a slight expectation within me that a spiritual blessing was about to happen, but thinking that it was only because of my procedure and my expectations of my pain finally going to be resolved, I kept up the silent prayer and meditation on the word. Earlier in the morning I had been reading Paul's experience before getting to the Island of Melita, in Acts 27 while listening to the motivational preacher on YouTube infer that it was a detour that was meant to happen, one of those things he said that the devil was using to steal, kill and destroy Paul's joy, but God was using it for his good.

Jean-Luc, I must say today you made it into my book and I use this moment to once more pray for you and your family, may you be strengthened and find a renewed love for God in your heart so that by this you will know that God never leaves anyone behind. He uses unique experiences like this one to reinforce the love He has for mankind and as long as we truly search Him out, He shows that He is knocking at the door. The only question that remains is: will we open up to His love?

His love for us may be understood just a bit more by those who keenly like to watch the stars and all the beauty of His creation around. They are the ones who can testify to this truth and by that understanding will then be able to grasp the length, breadth and depth of His love for us...

In fact, I was amazed that as far back as five thousand years ago people were always amazed at tagging at the stars, so much so that the grouping of them into stellar constellations was something passed down from the original Babylonians, Egyptians and Mesopotamians of the Bible, though the devil would have us believe more in the made-up stories of Greek mythology. However, I have a few stories of my own, which I discovered while reading and studying today. I hope that the Holy Spirit will help us discern and see this. You see, when Apostle Paul landed in Crete he had already passed through Jerusalem and had been assured there by the Lord that he, Paul, must testify of Him, the Lord in Rome. So, Paul was not just babbling when he was telling his fellow commuters (funny because he was the prisoner, but they were the captains, crew and centurion) that he perceived that there may be some damage to the ship and even to their lives if heed is not taken to the word of God. But even in the midst of this storm, which did, of course, hit, Paul was unfazed because, truth be told, he knew he would not die, but rather go to Rome to testify of God, as revealed by his stoic stance in Acts 28 when the beast of a viper tried to kill him.

My friend, today I ask, what is your purpose on this sea called life? Are you trying to be like the centurion and play it safe by going with the crowd and believing those who are more experienced in their worldly ways of doing things than trusting in the Godly way? Or are you like those whom Paul came across in Melita, who at one point, because of the snake that tried to bite Paul by clinging unto his hand as he tried to light a fire (being the prisoner and perhaps still in chains) was accused of being a murderer by the villagers, until he shook off the viper and immediately was pronounced a god? How much power are you allowing to work in you?

As a young child, I used to love to read books, I believe that is why I developed such an inquisitive mind. I could hide myself in the toilet once I got home after school divulging an Enid Blyton book so no one would disturb me. Those were the best moments I remember about my childhood, so that by the time we could afford to and started having our kids we bought the whole collection of Secret Seven and Famous Five for the girls. I think only one of them at the time caught the bug though. However, when we had our son, we helped him find the magic of reading, first with the Tintin Series, because that was my husband's own favourite growing up and though it worked for a while with my son, he finally settled for the faster paced Rick Riordan's series and the Percy Jackson world of Greek mythology.

For my husband and I, it was all about exposing kids to the magic of reading and the power of words in books giving them an edge in life over most that do not read; but most importantly allowing them to tap into their most creative side – IMAGINATION. Reading is power and every aspect of appreciating and comprehending literature in my opinion should be the first responsibility in nurture and care of a child. To this day I look forward to Friday evenings in this place, because those are the only days now in my adult life that I can dedicate to reading a novel. So, in effect my toilet is now associated with Friday evening readings. My kids know that and they see it and I am glad that all three now have caught the reading bug. It is a trait I am glad to have passed over and I hope that in the next generation when they start having their own kids, I would have a house in the south of France where they can come and pick out with their kids all the books that I have acquired and then relax and read to their heart's content. A haven of discussion by the fireplace on cold winter nights, discussing anything from politics to *The Tiger Who Came to Tea.*

Part 3:
The Ending

Jeremiah 33

Chapter 7
Corybantic

Sometimes that's all we've got left. It's the penultimate day of this challenge I set for myself at the beginning of November to be able to write fifty thousand words in thirty days. No small feat, right? So far, I'm behind by some thirty odd thousand words (smile). Yes, I have come to the realization that this challenge to write was a means to cause us to start writing in the first place. For us to jump in unrestrained and pour all our minds and might into creating the masterpiece of our dreams. Perhaps I could start all over again, but for me there is no such resolve. Instead I choose to press on and create a semblance of what was proposed for November...

No cooking.

No cleaning.

No running errands.

Doing absolutely nothing, except create by writing.

December seems the best time for this right? I ask my alter ego: Bella. She tells me, "Yes, throw yourself into reckless abandon mode and really go for it dear. Who's there to stop you?"

Hmmm! Back on track and feeling kind of happy with myself for tripping the guilt I can now go back to cruise control and revisit the weather here in Antibes. For you see it's been actually a very dreary November. Flash rains, gloomy skies and floods that have left homes in desperate need of insurance funds to cover the damage the water caused in the wake of its rainy deluge. I thought that would have made me sit and write, but no, each time I tried I got distracted by the cold. It was as if my brain was in a freeze and the words trapped in my cerebrum somehow that I could make no meaningful connections or remember sequence of events that I wanted to share in the book.

These are the seasons of this beautiful land – Antibes. Now the sun is out, and very much unlike the weekend before parents are happy to watch their kids play out in the sunshine, though, yes, with a twist – ha-ha windy!

After the mad pouring rain of last weekend that saw some 15 cm of water deposited in some gardens and garages, this weekend we have the cold, winter winds blowing in and with it for sure like I saw in the distance more beautiful deposits of snow in the mountains of the Alpes.

It's December and the sunshine continues to dazzle and sparkle so much that I cannot remember so much how it was like last month. Isn't that life, it almost feels like I'm an Israelite…(smile) when things are all good we applaud and feel good, praising and chanting hallelujah, but one small storm and we start to blame and complain, then the praises stop. Hmmm! Like Paul long time ago penned, who can save us from this wretched body and mind. What can we do to not behave like our three-year-old selves (another hearty smile); because, for the first time, I really know the answer. It is to live perpetually in gratitude. Yes, I know some may say, so simple and yes, it is actually so simple but because it is just that, many will not try it; or they may try it for a while and then stop. You know why? Yes, you got it a lack of perseverance when the immediate results don't start showing. It took me eight long years to figure this out and so when I write it down here I'm not just speaking from my head, but rather as one who has done a PhD would say, well researched!

I started a gratitude journal: the first time I wrote in it was the day my daughter turned ten, and now she is 22 and I still have space in that journal to write more… that's to show you how inconsistent I was at the beginning, but even though I would have seasons of stopping and starting – sometimes even years without writing in the book – this was all partly because from 2011 until about 2016, I had a super stressful job; however, I choose now to share just that first post with you, so you can trust what I say and you can make this journey of the seasons of your life in good faith that if you keep at gratitude it can only yield fruits of joy, peace, contentment, faith, patience and love for God.

05/05/2008

One day at a time: Thank you, Crystal is 10 today. Thank you, I am still able to play tennis and be good at it. Thank you for Jade who can do well staying by himself in the nursery. Thank you that I'm here in America living out my dreams to study and work in an effective manner. Thank you Lord for the means you provide every day that we might enjoy these things in Jesus' name. Amen.

31/12/2019

Dear book, nope December and January were certainly not the right months as I can testify since my last entry on this chapter; I have not had the time to spare to create instead I've been tuning things up at home with my two kids: the first and the last! But now everything is settled (smile) and Bella can get back to her writing, now the mom hat is temporarily hung and the kids are on some cruise control.

February 14 – the world again is in a frenzy celebrating yet another 'holiday' called Valentines. Who comes up with stuff like this? I'm perplexed but still I'm grateful to know I can write again with some reckless abandon. It's 21 degrees in the Var this afternoon and a perfect day to be out on the terrace of the newly minted Mouratoglou Hotel. What a journey, yes? Patrick has really been patient and persistent in getting his dreams; and being able to have front row seat to the unfolding of the events gives me great satisfaction, and, yes, hope for my dreams.

March 24 – Today as I took a shower I felt JOY because for the first time since that last entry, yes February 14, I have neither felt the desire or even an urge to write – I guess ha-ha the proverbial writer's block – so imagine my exhilarating gasp of relief when finally, as the hot water splashed on my shoulders I felt a lift within my whole being to get it going and I remembered the chapter where I wrote at the beginning doing absolutely nothing but create by writing. Funny right but that is where the whole world finds itself now. The government by decree has ordered its French citizens as of last night a complete sit at home allowing only one hour for a designated time for grocery shopping or exercise. Who would have thought it would ever come to this, but here we are in the 21st century forced by a virus that caught the populace off guard, but now threatening to bring the economy to its knees. Once more I say who would have thought? It's so distant a memory when I was walking the streets of Toulon and Fréjus and getting on a plane to Dubai for a wonderful week of chilling with my better half, only to arrive back here in France and within a week and a half shut-in to war-like confinement not to be able to go out for perhaps what may be seven weeks!

Borders between countries being shut all over the world in order to get a grip on the pandemic and at least buy the virologists some more time to understand and possibly procure an antidote to stem the already frightening numbers that succumb to this malady every day.

This time we are all fighting one common enemy, and for the first time in a while (even though it's only a small tiny glimmer) in these dark times, at least one can say we are all united, and for sure with the confinement steps taken by leaders of most countries around the world giving backseat to such matters as Syria (ISIS), Brexit and indeed the Trump impeachment that were seemingly taking up all the focus from everything else.

In coming together to fight ONE enemy, it is not yet clear how we shall emerge from this, neither do we know for how long it will linger, but the only thing I know as far as my eyes can see is that the world, as we know it, will never be the same again. We will no longer look upon each other as strangers because a 'war' such as this has shown us that we should really be our brothers' keepers first of all through a genuine love for ourselves. As we have come to realise in one week, by having good hygiene practices – yes, who could have thought, washing hands and keeping a safe distance – would one day save us from ourselves and help preserve the older generation – we can truly love our neighbour!

Chapter 8

"I have heard of Thee by the hearing of the ear: but now mine eye seeth Thee."

– Job 42:5

Who would have thought? I'd be saying this in April, Oui Avril! And we are still in quarantine mode. If someone had said to me six months ago that we will be at home – I mean everyone – with no hope of sharing a cup of coffee in a Boulangerie, I would have laughed and said, "You kidding, hell no! Not in the south of France," especially with the weather so nice and the sun so bright and shiny; but lo and behold This is the life we find ourselves living here and now in the year 2020.

Shortly in the next chapter we shall go down memory lane, as I draw to the end of this nice discussion with you my beautiful reader who's stayed with me still thus far: I will tell you of another April, a time in my life when things took an interesting turn in our family and changed us for good. Much like I believe this hibernation will change our world. Even when we don't see it, he is working and definitely when we don't feel it, he is still at work in us and through us. You never know when the dots connect, but one sure thing is that if you stay diligent at your post and remain true to the one thing that keeps haunting you then it all falls into place. Tennis has always been the pivot of the Nzewi household, at least as long as I can remember when my sister-in-law brought me a tennis racket on one of her early visits to Nigeria from the States. Who would have known that following my win at the 'Milo tennis tournament' in the parents' category would have sparked off a love that would lead to my daughter getting a college degree and my son studying at one of the most elite tennis academies in the south of France.

It's pretty silent around here. The afternoon breeze behind me, a lawn mower off in the distance and a barking dog on a terrace, these are the only sounds I hear as I walk from the Super U, next to my domain. I cannot complain one bit but rather I'm at peace, for now we know for sure we are going to be in confinement through to the end of April. President Macron made another impressive third broadcast and as usual he had me mesmerised (smile); it must be those puppy brown eyes, yes, for he had me nodding and agreeing that this was the best option for the country at this juncture. I felt like an eskimo being led to the market to get some snow and so looking forward to the journey. As I look into the horizon and see the distant houses tucked in the hills of Golfe Juan, I remember that it was only about eight Thursday's to the day that I had planned for a trip to Vallauris to see the ceramic museum of the great Picasso. I was planning that during the school holidays I will give Jade a tour of pottery and explain to him the verse: "As clay is in the hand of the potter so are we in the Father's hands." What an oxymoron: the cruel kindness I will say of these times we are in.

You see, on the one hand, there are people struggling for their lives in hospitals, those in care homes also living in fear not knowing what their future holds; but on the other hand, here I am being grateful and actually saying thank God for the stillness of everything. Finally, I can write in peace. I can come out to the gardens in my domain and fully enjoy it. I mean fully, fully know what it is to allow your creative juices flow and cascade into the pages of the book I am writing to create the piece I've always wanted.

I'm meditating without any pressure for time. I can do the full three-hour meditation and stretch for an hour without rushing into the next activity.

My body is being fully rejuvenated. I'm connecting with family members on levels that I have not done in years and finally becoming still as I knew I should have two years ago.

I am truly becoming AWARE and somehow, I know I do not speak for myself alone, for there are also those becoming aware of their inner selves because that is what comes automatically when we study God's word and come in contact with the awesome energy and power of the great creator – Jesus Christ – in His Gospel He tells us that on a certain day we will come to the realization that as He is in His Father, we are in Christ so is He in us! And for me that reality came this week. I knew for sure that before now I only heard of God and was looking through a stained glass, but now in reality by my very own self confinement within the imposed confinement I have and am continually seeing God like job said after all his solitary experiences – "… But now mine eye seeth thee."

Chapter 9

"He restoreth my soul: He leadeth me in the paths of righteousness for His name's sake!"

– Psalm 23:3

So, this book is finally taking a twist of its own without me being in total control. Funny how we start off somewhere thinking that we know exactly what we want or what we are doing, only to be exposed a few days or years, or even in this instance, a few chapters worth of time that we truly had no inkling of what it was that we had to say or were about to discuss in the first place. So, we go into talking about others just so the spot light is not on us, as if talking about the others will make us feel better about ourselves, or give us a sense of solidarity in the fact that we are not alone. This is one of the very reasons I love sports, more so tennis; because this game is surely a microcosm of life and it is even so much better because the term given to a really good thrashing on the tennis court is called a 'love game'. Can you imagine? I'd like to know who came up with such twisted humour. I get bageled on the tennis court and when asked what the score is all my opponent will say is "love – love," with a grim smile on his face. That was the score of yesterday's game at the ongoing TenPro Tournament taking up my writing time.

Since the beginning of 2018 when I decided to quit my job of 15 odd years and focus on the tennis career of my young son. Is this legal? I mean what does a 12-year-old know about being professional, let alone playing tennis at a professional level. This is just a means to having him get focused and start taking interest in something; for up to this moment, he just seems to be okay with drifting from one thing to the other without any full commitment to any sport, subject or chore. It is okay when you are nine (according to my unwritten book on parenting); however, there's something about turning double digits that simply speaks of having a certain passion or inkling for something. In his case a small spark set off in the game of tennis, though actually he had started playing since the time he turned six weeks as a foetus (smile) is worth holding unto. Yes, perhaps it was something I passed on while sitting up late watching with my husband many years ago when Novak Djokovic just hit the scenes in the mid part of the dominance of Federer somewhere in between 2006 and early 2007. After dominating for about three years almost unchallenged save for Nadal and only on clay at that, comes this young boy/child Novak who took the Rogers Cup title match to the then defending champion – Federer. I remember watching that sweet victory, coming out firing and surprising Roger by taking the first set in a very well contested tie break (7/2), then recollecting himself after a 2/6 second set to snatch the victory in another nail-biting third set deciding tie break (7/2); and praying that my newly born baby boy would one day contend for a cup like this and defeat a player of such calibre.

Such were the thoughts going through my mind yesterday as I watched another 12-year-old with an identical backhand as Roger Federer, tall and lanky with such confidence in his serve, contend against my smallish son, who, in contrast, came on court looking tired and drained of all energy, but still I prayed and felt optimistic that the events unfolding before my eyes would somehow replay as the above I just recalled. It was not to be so – we took the love defeat and settled it in our minds to wait for another performance in the evening. Tennis is a very wonderful sport and if given the opportunity I could preach a whole sermon of how this is the sport of angels. From the serve position, which is a poise similar to the hallelujah posture with hands high up and head looking to the skies, one can immediately tell how much majestic the game is! The name given it from time immemorial is the gentleman's game because of the elite nature of its history. However, as with most sports now, it has been opened up to a field of young talents from all over and all works of life and along with that has the great physicality and requirements to play the game increased. So, as we sit to watch the evening game yesterday, against a bigger and taller opponent, I pray once more for my son.

The weather as predicted becomes so chilly that I can hear my ears ring from the cold. I go inside to the cafeteria to get a cup of coffee and imagine that if this match turns out to be a long one, then I would be drinking a lot of coffee throughout just to stay warm. Again, he starts the match more or less like a slow motion and I wonder to myself would this be another 'love game'? Soon the first set is over 6/2 and the coach and

I are left wondering why this guy who had played so well this past two days at practice was failing. Could it be that it wasn't yet his season? In retrospect, I think this is the only logical answer to what has perplexed me in the last 24 hours since he played his last two matches. The second set was different however, and he played a better match, coming up with some magical shots but more importantly putting up a fight. He decided to take the game to his opponent and was eventually able to wrestle a break when it mattered to keep himself in the match towards the end although it was a little too late, as he eventually surrendered his own serve to end the second set 6/4.

In a way, I am glad for the rains that came today, because it gave us both time to sit and reflect. Like I mentioned earlier, I love this game so much because it is a microcosm of life. Each moment I take up the racket to serve, I am in awe of the God I serve, I lift up my hands like I did today as I practiced serve and let out my frustrations on the ball. It felt so good and reminded me why this is one of the very purest forms of my communication with God. Today I knew I needed to play tennis even though I had thought I should not, but it was like a force pushing me to prepare to play with my group (after two weeks of break), and after my collagen injection two days prior to correct the arthrosis on my hip joint. It was the perfect timing for me and all the drills were on point. The coaches, Nannete and Robyn, were just what my emotions and ego needed and I believe the Holy Spirit used that one hour session to restore my soul. The action of leading and restoring is a continual one and a ritual that goes on daily for the soul that allows the Holy Spirit to be in charge of his or her life. And this is what I have come to find out in the time I have spent in France. This beautiful country makes me come face to face with God in the seasons of my life.

A Time to Reflect

When I am feeling optimistic and happy, I raise a hallelujah to the Lord by singing in the mountains that are all around me, and when I feel sad and see myself going into some dark misty place, I go to the valley or just stare at the sea about me, or simply bury my head in the pillow knowing full well that when I awake right here in my domain surrounding me are the beautiful fleurs of Domaine Juan Fleur. The well-kept flowers in their different colours remind me at these dark moments that there is beauty in the world, if we look out for it. Have you noticed that when you smile at a perfect stranger and nod your head as you pass each other along the way, the person is forced to reciprocate the action? So, it is with the vibes we so often unknowingly send around us each day; and trust me this is no feel-good mumbo-jumbo psychological kind of stuff because it is an experiment I carried out some time ago when I started actually paying attention. Some years ago, I bought a book called 'The Secret' and shortly after that watched a short video on the same theme about how we draw to ourselves what it is we constantly are thinking about. Being the scientist that I am and also the true student of the Bible, I said to myself at that point: it can't get worse than this, right? So, I started writing every day what it was I was grateful for each time, and before long I began to always truly feel grateful, now I cannot tell for instance how long I did this before the change came, hence that proves that it works because it was in the action and the everyday feelings of gratitude to God for everything. He placed in my way – either good or bad – I tried always to find a nugget to be thankful for and gradually this became my attitude. I know for a certainty that since I have been in Juan Les Pins I have never one day not been grateful to God for the elements. The weather, which I don't fully understand right now and the language, but slowly and surely, I am beginning to get a hang of both and just being assured of the fact that I will comprehend it fully one day makes me full of more gratitude to the one who has brought me here to enjoy the land.

Now as a family, tennis is the pivotal vehicle for which our mission here on Earth is revolving and that for me could not have been more appropriate because in case you have not noticed by now, I kind of eat, sleep and breathe tennis. Perhaps the only other people on this planet that do it more than me are the very ones I am now spending most of my days with. Isn't that funny and again going to prove my point that what we think about and what we most earnestly yearn for we draw to ourselves? Who would have thought a lowly, lecturer's daughter from Nigeria will eventually marry another humble, God fearing lecturer's son and after 20 years, move to the south of France to provide a life for their kids, and play tennis at the most elite level! It is truly amazing and worth spending hours on end praising God for, which by the way I do. However, the gist of the book will not be complete if I do not take a step back to start the story from the very beginning. From April to August of 2007.

It was the evening of March 11 and I remember being normal – if you can call seven months pregnant female with indigestion anytime she eats normal. I had been previously pregnant with girls, two for that matter before this last (oops!); my surprise blessing hence one of the middle names being Uchechukwu – meaning God's plan. Yeah, Drake, your song would have been 'Uchechukwu' had it been released in Nollywood. Anyway, so there I was after having my dinner sitting and watching the March ATP 1000 Masters Indian Wells semi-finals and this was right about the time that Andy Murray and Novak were beginning to become a buzz, little did we know at the time that they will be named among the greats of tennis; but I remember one day early in 2007 having watched Novak play in Adelaide, Australia wining that tournament amidst tough opposition, I instinctively knew that he would be one of the players to watch out for and commenting to my husband that at last I had found a young champion we can back, because until that moment we both had not agreed on the key tennis player for our family enjoyment. So, coming back to the match between Novak Djokovic and Andy, while watching these two young lads play their hearts out and give all their best, I remember touching my protruding stomach and saying to myself – still believing that I was months away from delivery – that in two months when this bundle of joy arrives (for we already knew we were having our first boy), he would one day play like these two guys and give me great happiness. Such was the passion I had then and to this day still carry when I watch a good tennis match, be it on the ATP tour, the WTA, a practice match or just a pick up recreational game between my husband and his friends at the club.

Man can plan, but ultimately God has the final say in our lives, all we mortals can do is pray that every day we have breath that we do move in His will, and for me this is exactly what happened in the next four days following that Saturday evening. For on the 14th while speaking on the phone with my husband who happened to be on another continent at the time getting ready to go to work, while I was getting ready for bed, I felt my first contraction; and given this had happened before in the course of this pregnancy, I didn't know if to take it seriously or let it slide. After all, I thought I am not new at this pregnancy thing so… But immediately I got off the phone with him I called my Aunt who happened to be at work at the time, at the Methodist Hospital, Houston downtown and she came to pick me up at 11 pm that night. I truly could not believe that the little boy was coming into this world at this time. He is way too early, it's only 31 weeks Lord, and I am not ready for this. But in His time He makes all things perfect, and though for that season of our lives after his birth and for the immediate months that followed being in the ICU for a month before taking him home and only being able to visit during the day and call the nurses at night because of course we had to leave each day to pick up and take care of our other two daughters who were in the third and second grades respectively, I can say that we grew closer and got to know our limits; for my husband and I were really pushed both physically and emotionally in that time.

The day in April he came out of the hospital, I remember saying to my husband as we passed the Lee Le Clear Public Tennis Centre that I wanted to stop and just hit some tennis balls, knowing fully well that prior to that week we had spent the weekend watching the Clay Court Houston Open played for the last time at our club the Westside Tennis And Fitness Club, totally immersing ourselves in the atmosphere even getting the Bryan Brothers and Ivo Karlovic to sign a ball for the little boy, and having the girls take a picture with Venus Williams. It was indeed a time of bonding, happiness and the joy of truly knowing the mercy and grace of God are sufficient for even what some may see from the outside as the worst times of one's life. At this moment as I come to the end of this chapter of our lives and the dawning of a new season of love, laughter and tennis, I am optimistic that the journey thus far will culminate in the expectations of our dreams. For as I mentioned at the very beginning: the future belongs to those who believe (and by this, I mean consistently strive for and see it in front of them) in the beauty of their dreams.